Windows 8

51 Essential Tips for Windows 8 Beginners!

By: Aubrey Mitchell

Disclaimer

The author assumes no liability for advice or suggestions offered in this book. The author and publisher of this book and the accompanying materials have used their best efforts in preparing this book. The author and publisher make no representation or warranties with respect to the accuracy, applicability, fitness, or completeness of the contents of this book. The information contained in this book is strictly for informational purposes. Therefore, if you wish to apply ideas contained in this book, you are taking full responsibility for your actions.

Table of Contents

Introduction

More than 75 percent of the world's computers are run on Windows operating system. Because of this, Microsoft has to come out with the next best thing. In comes Windows 8. Windows 8 has revolutionized the way users experience

 desktop s. It was released in 2012 and is probably the most

flexible, adaptable and user-friendly Windows Operating System ever.

The largest change, and the one you notice first, is that the desktop is gone. When you first go to use Windows 8, it will seem entirely alien with flat tiles and bright colors. While the desktop is there, in the background, the Start Screen is what you are taken to when you first boot your PC.

It's a whole new ballgame with Windows 8, as many of the features and commands are hidden – even the more common ones. There are new ways to launch programs (or what are now called apps) as well as new ways to organize your apps. It will definitely take getting used to, but Windows 8 is likely one of the best OS Microsoft has come out with so far.

Whether you've just purchased a new computer with Windows 8, you've upgraded to Windows 8 or would just like to learn about the OS before you do the upgrade, this eBook is going to give you 50 of the best and most valuable Windows 8 tips that will help you learn the new operating system, find your way around, and access some of the best features.

With time, patience and the following 50 tips, you'll begin to feel like you're at home with Windows 8 rather than a foreign exchange student in someone's home. So, let's get started!

Chapter 1: Getting the Ball Rolling

Since Windows 8 is probably the largest change that Microsoft has ever made, there are definitely new things to learn. This first chapter will focus on getting a little bit more familiar with the new

layout and basic navigation help.

Tip #1: Understanding the Charms Bar

The Charms bar is a menu that you'll probably use a million times, if not more, throughout the time that you have Windows 8 on your PC. It contains five charms (icons): Search, Share, Start, Devices, and Settings. Alternatively, you can use the Windows key and the letter C to open up the Charms bar. You can also use your mouse to open it up by hovering over the bottom or top right side of the screen. If you choose to switch to the Desktop version instead of using the new Windows 8 Start Screen, then the Charms bar won't be of much use to you.

Tip #2: Opening the Control Panel

Users that are new to Windows8 will likely find it a bit difficult to locate the Control Panel, as it can't be accessed the way it was in previous versions of Windows. And contrary to what you may think, you won't find it under Settings via the Charms bar. Now, there are three different ways you can access the Control Panel. If you decide to use the Desktop rather than the Start screen (discussed later), then you have two options: Press Windows and the letter I or you can right click in the lower left part of the screen, you'll open up the Quick Access menu and Control Panel appears directly underneath Task Manager.

Tip #3: Using Quick Access
Because Windows 8 has eliminated the traditional Start menu in the bottom left-hand corner of the screen; however, there is a Quick Access menu that you can open up from the same location. Go to where the Start Menu generally is and right click with your mouse. Alternatively, you can use your keyboard by pressing and holding the X and Windows key. The menu that will appear will offer a variety of options, such as Control Panel, Search Dialog, Device Manager, Explorer and more.

Tip #4: Displaying All Apps
In order to find and display all of your downloaded applications on your computer,

you'll want to press and hold the Ctrl and Tab keys. Alternatively, you can swipe up from the bottom of your computer screen or click the arrow button that you see at the very bottom left of your screen. Once you do this, you'll see all of your apps displayed. If you do not see the app or program that you are looking for, simply start typing it in.

Tip #5: Closing an App

If you've already been trying to us your new Windows 8 computer, then you may have

 noticed that there aren't X's at the top left of the screen to close programs. The apps that you use are suspended once you begin using a different app so that it doesn't drain your system. When your computer does finally need those resources that the suspended apps are using, they'll close out automatically.

However, it is possible close down the programs yourself. All you need to do it move your mouse cursor up to the top of the computer screen. The cursor should turn into a hand. Once this happens, hold down the left button on your

mouse and drag it down. The program should then shrink into the size of a thumbnail that can be closed by dragging it away from the screen. If you don't want to deal with all that, you can press the F4 and Alt keys. Of course, there's also Ctrl+Shift+Esc, which will launch your Task Manager. In the Apps list, select the program you'd like to close, right click it and select "End Task".

Tip #6: Shutting It Down

Because the traditional start menu is gone, some users may find it difficult to shut down their computer. It's actually quite easy. All you have to do is take your cursor to bottom right hand portion of the screen. Choose settings and a menu will appear that has a Power button. Once you click on the Power button, you will select Shut Down (or Restart). You can still use the Ctrl+Alt+Del option as well as Alt+F4.

Tip #7: Shut Down in a Single Click

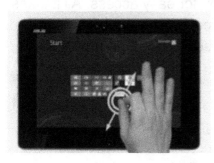

While it isn't necessarily difficult to shut your PC down, some people may prefer to use the mouse once with one click in order to shut down their PC. Well, this can easily be made to happen. Windows 8 makes it so that you can create your very own power off button so that you don't have to go through the multiple-step process, as defined above, in order to shut down your computer.

You're going to want to first create a desktop shortcut by right clicking, highlighting New and choosing Shortcut. You will want to enter the following text with no quotation marks: "shutdown /s /t 0" for the location and name your shortcut Shutdown. Select Finish.

Now that your shortcut is made, right click on it and select Properties. Under the tab that is labeled Shortcut, choose Change Icon and select okay. Choose your desired icon, such as a Power button since it makes the most sense. Then, right click the desktop shortcut once again and select the option to Pin to Start. This will give you the ability to place the icon anywhere on your Start screen for easy access. All it takes is one click of this icon from the Start screen and your computer will successfully shut down.

Tip #8: Using Semantic Zoom

Your Start Screen is not full of big, bold tiles that represent your programs and apps. When you put these into groups, they're easy to see. However, what if you have hundreds of programs and apps installed? You won't be able to see the vast majority of them – unless of course you want to scroll and scroll and scroll some more. Luckily, Windows 8 created the semantic zoom. This feature can be used on touch screen and non-touch screen monitors. For mouse and keyboard users, hold down on the Ctrl button and use the wheel on your mouse to zoom in and zoom out. For touch screen users, use your fingers to squeeze and un-squeeze to view your programs.

Tip #9: Easy Access to Startup Items

Previously in Windows, you had to run the MSConfig command program in order to access the startup programs. Now, this is no longer necessary. All you have to do is simply pull up the Task Manager with Ctrl+Alt+Del. Once you've entered the Task Manager, simply select the tab that says More Details at the bottom and then choose the Startup tab from the top of the screen. You can then enable and disable startup programs.

Tip #10: Sync a Microsoft Account

Although a local user account is fine, it definitely makes things easier if you have Microsoft account linked to your PC. In order to connect yours, pull up the Charms bar, go to Settings and then Change PC Settings. Select Users and then Switch to a Microsoft account. Enter in your account details, or create one, and customize the settings to sync.

Tip #11: Going Directly to the Desktop

Many Windows 8 users avoid the new Start Screen colorful tiles, so if this is something that you want to do here's how to boot your computer directly to the desktop instead of the Windows 8 Start Screen. Simply right click on the taskbar and go to Properties and then Navigation. Check the box next to "When I sign in or close all apps on a screen, go to the desktop instead of Start". Click OK. Voila, you won't see those vivid tiles ever again – unless you want to.

Chapter 2: Let's Get Personal

Windows 8 has a number of new options that allow customization and personalization that previous versions of Windows did not have. This chapter will help you take advantage of these new features so that your new Windows computer can truly be your own.

Tip #12: Change the Size of Your Tiles

If you don't like the default size of your tiles, you

can change them. Right click one of the app buttons or press and hold the tile. A gray bar will pop up at the bottom of the computer screen with several options. One of the options listed is "Resize". Tap or click on this button to proceed. A pop-up menu with several options will appear. You can select Small, Medium, Large or Wide tiles. Once you select the desired size, your tile will change.

Tip #13: Customize Your Account Picture

You need to open the Charms bar to change your account picture. In order to do this, swipe from the right side of your screen or use your mouse and take the cursor down to the bottom right corner. Then choose Change PC Settings. On the left hand side of the screen, several options will appear and you will want to select the Accounts tab. Here, you will see your current picture. Underneath this thumbnail will be a button that says Browse. You want to click on this to find your new picture. Select your new picture and press Choose Image.

Tip #14: Customize Your Wallpaper

Normally, a person's computer wallpaper has some sort of significant meaning. In some cases, it is just a beautiful background that the user likes. Whatever the case is, if you want to personalize your wallpaper so that it isn't a dreary old traditional Windows background, here's how you can do it. Open the Charms bar and select Settings. Next, you will want to select Personalize. The Personalize screen will appear and it has three primary areas. The top and first area contains several selections of Windows-supplied wallpaper screens. Select the one that stands out. Next, if you would like to, you can go to the second section and change the color of the wallpaper. The bottom section is also a color change for the details and accent of the wallpaper.

Tip #15: Customize Your Lock Screen

More than likely, you have a picture of your kids on the lock screen of your phone or MP3 player (if you don't have kids, maybe you have your favorite car, boyfriend/girlfriend or your favorite celebrity). Now, you can do this with your computer. When you go to unlock your computer, instead of seeing some general picture that isn't attractive in any way, you can now used a snapshot of your family, pet, loved one or your favorite place.

In order to add your own photo to the lock screen, you need to pull up the Charms bar. Choose Settings and then Change PC Settings. Now, select PC and Devices from the top of the right hand subheading list. There will be several options listed here, but the lock screen is the first one. Select Browse to peruse through your photos and files on your PC to choose the one that you would now like to be your lock screen.

Tip #16: Modify Notifications on Your Lock Screen

Just as you can see notifications on your cell phone without unlocking it, you can now see notifications on your PC without unlocking it. In order to modify the notifications that you will actually be able to see on your lock screen – and the ones that you can't – you need to open up your Charms bar yet once again. Select Settings and then Change PC Settings. From here, you will go to General and then Lock Screen. Now, you need to go down to the subheading that says Lock Screen Applications. App symbols will not appear in boxes. Some will be pre-populated and some will simply be labeled with a plus sign. The ones with the plus sign are so that you can add apps to receive notifications. Click the plus sign to open up a list of apps that you can choose from. Select the app you would like to receive notifications from on your lock screen.

Tip #17: Categorizing and Naming Your Apps

If you start collecting app after app and pin sites as tiles, you will create a huge mess on your Start screen that you likely won't even be able to sift through and find what you need. Luckily, Windows 8 comes with some organizational tools that are built-in and can help you organize things a bit so that when you need to find a particular app, you can do so quickly and easily.

To get started, drag the tiles that you would like into the same group to the far right side of the screen. Windows 8 will make sure these are placed appropriately. When you have all your tiles assembled and are content with your gathering, use semantic zoom (which is described in just a moment as Tip #9) to zoom out and view your desktop easily. Right click with your mouse on the group of tiles that you just recently assembled and click on "Name Group" so that you can name the group.

Now, continue doing this until you have all of your apps in appropriate groups and are happy with the way everything looks.

Chapter 3: Being Productive

This chapter is going to focus on tips that will help you be more productive and organized. You will begin to see that some things with Windows 8 are familiar, even though there are plenty of things that are completely alien to you. There are a lot of things that your new operating system

 can do and many of these things will be explained within this chapter.

Tip #18: Using Apps Side-by-Side

Most programs will use the entire screen while running; however, Windows 8 makes it possible for more than one app to be viewed and used on the screen at the same time. Depending on the width of your computer screen, you may be able to view more than two apps at the same time. For two apps, your screen needs to be at minimum 1,366 pixels. For three apps, your screen needs to be at more than 1,500 pixels.

All it takes is to drag one app to one side of the screen by going to the top of the screen and waiting for the cursor to turn into a hand. Locate your next app on the Start screen or go to the left side of the screen to choose one of the currently running programs and do the same with it.

Tip #19: Pinning Websites to the Start Screen

If you have a website that you use frequently, especially on a daily basis, you may want to Pin it to the Start Screen for easier access. It sure beats having to type in the URL every time, right? In order to pin a website to the Start screen, you will need to first open up the website in Internet Explorer. On the bottom right side of the screen, you will see a little thumbtack inside a circle. Click this and a small pop-up menu will appear at which time you will select Pin to Start. You can then Change or Confirm the name of the tile before actually Pinning it. It will now be at the far right side of your Start Screen.

Tip #20: Pinning Programs for Easy Access

If there is an app or program that you use frequently and you don't want to have to pull up the entire list of apps and search for the program every time you need to use, there is an easier way. All you have to do is pin it to the Start Menu. Access all of your apps and start typing it the program that you want to pin. Once it appears, right click it and select the "Pin to Start" option. Alternatively, you can press and hold the program/app icon and select the "Pin to Start" option. Now, it will appear at the far right end of the Start Screen.

Tip #21: Automatically Log In

As long as you don't mind losing your administrative privileges, you can set it so that your computer will automatically log in when your reboot your computer so that you don't have to every single time. In order to do this, press the Windows and R keys, type "netplwiz" and then hit Enter so that the User Accounts menu is launched. Uncheck the box for "Users must enter a user name and password to use the computer" and then hit OK. Then, simply type in your username and password. Press OK. Restart your computer and when your computer restarts, your Start screen should automatically launch.

Tip #22: Install a Start Menu

If you can't stand the thought of not having a Start Menu to work with every day, then you can get it back completely by downloading and installing the Classic Shell app. Once installed, you'll be able to see and use the standard start menu. You will see the search box, Recent Items, shut down options and more.

Tip #23: Photo Viewer by Default

Unless you change it, photos that you click on will not automatically open up in Windows Photo Viewer, as most users prefer. Thankfully, it's an easy fix. Open the Charms bar, and type Default into the Search bar. Select Default from the search results and then Default Programs. Now click on Set Default Programs. Scroll down to find Windows Photo View in the list of Programs. Click on "Set this program to default".

Tip #24: Search Everywhere with Smart Search, Or Not

Start typing anything you want from the Start screen. As you do this, documents and files that match on the computer will begin to appear as well as web results from Bing. Click a link to visit it. It can prove to be very useful in some instances, but in other cases, it can quite annoying. So, if this isn't a feature that you like, you can easily disable it so that it won't be a nuisance. Simply open the Charms Bar, select Settings, then Change PC Settings, select Search and change "Use Bing to search online" from On to Off.

Tip #25: Give Your PC an Energy Boost

Unlike previous versions of Windows, Windows 8 allows users to refresh the system without having to do a backup and without losing any data. To do this, open up the Settings and select the Change PC Settings option at the bottom. Go to the General tab and select to get started with the "Refresh Your PC without affecting your files" option about mid-way down. Click Refresh. After a several minutes (it can take as much as 15 minutes, depending on the amount of data that is currently on your PC), your computer will reboot itself and you'll be starting with a fresh system while still having every single one of your files that you wanted to keep safe.

Tip #26: Using the Reading View

If you're using the Start Screen Mode, then you'll be able to use the new enhanced Reading View feature. Located on the right side of the address bar in Internet Explorer is a chunky book – it only shows up when viewing certain pages. Click on this icon to experience the Reading View feature. With this feature, you have no advertisements or anything else blocking you from simply reading the material on the page. Simply tap the book again in order to return to the regular web view.

Chapter 4: Safety & Security

Your PC's security should be of utmost importance. Without a fully protected system, your computer can become a cluttered mess of viruses and threats that could wreak havoc on your entire system and life. In order to better protect your PC, your data and yourself, there are a number of new security settings that can be utilized with Windows 8. Don't forget, security goes well beyond protecting your PC from malicious threats, as Windows 8 allows you to manage protect data with custom passwords. Ultimately, this chapter is going to talk about features and tips to use that will ensure you have a safe and secure place to work or play.

Tip #27: Setting Up Windows Firewall

Setting up your firewall is the first line of defense and is the first tip in this chapter. Launch the Search charm and search for Firewall. Select Windows Firewall in order to pull up the security settings for the Firewall. Select "Turn Windows Firewall on or off" and make sure your Public and Private network firewalls are turned on. For both, select the box next to "Notify Me" and press OK.

In the Firewall Settings, you can also restrict or allow certain apps. Click on "Allow an app or feature through Windows Firewall". Choose the desired apps.

Tip #28: Adjusting Basic Privacy Settings

Many of your apps will have default privacy settings; however, this may not float your boat, if you will. Your computer has access to a large amount of sensitive, personal data, from pictures and videos to your name and location. In order to make adjustments to these settings, you will need to press the letter I key and the Windows key, then select Change PC Settings. From here, you'll select the Privacy option on the left hand side of the screen and go on to personalize the privacy settings to your liking.

Tip #29: Setting Up a Picture Password

 Instead of having to deal with a complex alphanumeric password, Windows 8 introduces a new concept for security: picture passwords. You can now use a picture as your password. To set it up, you need to press the Windows key and the letter I key in order to open up the settings. Choose to change the PC settings, which is located at the bottom right. Go to the tab that says Users. Underneath the Sign In Options, you'll see the option to create a picture password. Here, you will be able to select the picture of your choice and then define three (not two and not four) gestures on the image to work as your password. These gestures can be clicks, swipes or circles. You will have to repeat your gestures in order to confirm the new picture password that you have set. Once you are finished, select Finish. The next time that you log into your account, you will have to use this new picture password to gain access.

Tip #30: File History Backup

If you want to keep your data and files secure on your computer, Windows 8 creates a new security feature known as file history backup. Keep in mind that you will need another internal hard drive or an external hard drive that the backup can be saved to. You can even use a USB flash drive if you want. In order to get started with File History Backup, you'll need to plug in your external hard drive, flash drive, etc. and select the option "Configure this drive for backup using File History".

Next, you'll want to go to the Control Panel, then System and Security, and then File History. Here you can click on Exclude Folders to exclude certain folders from being backed up, Advanced Settings in order to choose the frequency of your backup, Change Drive to select the destination for the backup, and Turn On so that the file history backup feature is enabled and ready to go.

Tip #31: Stay Current with Windows Updates Alerts

If you don't frequently shut down or log off of your computer, then you won't ever hear of Windows Updates, regardless of how important they are. The only time Windows Update alerts show up on Windows 8 is when you first log on. Luckily, developers have gone above and beyond and created a few quick fixes for this.

Two of the most popular free tools to add that "updates are available" notification back to your system tray are: Windows Update Notification Tool and Windows Update Notifier.

Tip #32: Parental Controls

If your computer is being shared with your children, then you will want to use the new and helpful Windows 8 feature that allows child accounts to be set up for family safety. You can block certain websites and even set time limits  for computer usage. You can keep up with everything that is being accessed and viewed while keeping tabs on all of their computer browsing activity. You can block your kids from gambling to restricting the usage of certain sites and apps.

Pull up the Charms bar and choose Settings, then Change PC Settings and then Accounts. Choose Other Accounts and click on "Add a user account" and then click on "Add a child's account". You can use an e-mail or choose not to use an e-mail when setting the child account up. Provide the necessary information and click

Next. Now, you'll need to confirm the information you just entered and click Finish. The account will now appear under Other Accounts.

In order to edit the permissions, click on the search icon next to Accounts and search for Family. Go to Family Safety and select the computer user you would like to adjust permissions for. Find Web Filtering underneath Windows Settings. Here, you can adjust all the settings from app restrictions and time limits to blocking preferences and web filtering. You can also click on User Information to view Activity Reports.

Tip #33: Stay Safe with SmartScreen

This is a built-in feature with Windows 8 that's provides your PC with an added layer of security when it comes to malicious and unrecognized apps and files. SmartScreen will notify you if an

 app or file isn't malicious and will prevent it from running so that no damage is done to your computer. You can modify the settings to alert you or not to alert you by opening the Control Panel, then Action Centre, and select to Windows SmartScreen Settings. You can choose to keep the warning

that requires approval by an administrator before downloading, keep the warning but avoid needing administrator approval or disable the warnings all together. Make your selection and press OK.

Tip #34: Booting in Safe Mode

Like previous versions, Windows 8 allows users to start their computer in Safe Mode in order to troubleshoot any major problems. While you can pull up the MSConfig command, there is an easier way to access Safe Mode. Open up the Charm bar, select Settings, and then Change PC Settings. From here, you'll want to click on the tab that says General. Scroll all the way to the very bottom and click the Restart icon, which you'll see under Advanced Startup. This will launch an Advanced Options Boot Menu. Choose Troubleshoot, then Advanced Options, and then Startup Settings. Now, you'll need to press Restart and you'll see a list of options appear. One of those options is to launch your computer in Safe Mode. Press the number for the option you would like to use and your computer will then reboot and enter Safe Mode.

Tip #35: Creating Tile for Safe Mode Boot

Because the above is a lot of labor, if you want to reduce some of that work, create its own tile. Right click on the desktop, select New and then select Shortcut. Now, you'll need to type in: "shutdown /r /o /t 0" without the quotation marks. Press Next and name the shortcut to your liking, although Safe Mode Start or something similar would be very appropriate. Your new tile will be at the far right side of the Start Screen. Once you click on it, you'll be taken straight to the Safe Mode Boot Menu.

Tip #36: App Usage History

The new Windows 8 task manager allows users to find out just how much time has been used per app. This information can be found by launching Task Manager and then going to App History. To clear all the compiled data, select Delete Usage History.

Chapter 5: Browsing the World Wide Web

Because the web browsing experience is completely different with Windows 8 than prior Windows OS, this chapter focuses solely on some of the new commands and features that

you'll come across and need.

Tip #37: Browsing with Tabs

Internet Explorer with Windows 8 permits multiple tab browsing. In order to have more than one web page up, which constitutes more than one tab, you need to right click a link and select the option to "Open link in new tab". In order to see all tabs that are open, right click on an empty part of the computer screen and a panel will appear at the bottom that shows thumbnails of the open tabs. To close one, click the X. Alternatively, to open one of those tabs, click on it. When the panel is open, there is a plus sign at the right hand side that will open up a blank tab and window so that you can search or open any link you'd like. The circle with the three dots inside it will allow you to open up a private window or reopen a previously closed tab.

Tip #38: How to Hide Your Tracks

Whether you're viewing something you shouldn't be (because, yes, every single page that is viewed in Internet Explorer is recorded and saved in the history), you want to clean out your cache or you simply want to boost your security, clearing your browser history is very easy. All you need to do is open up Internet Explorer. Move the cursor to the top left opening up the Charms bar, where you'll select Settings. Next, you'll click on Options and click on Select to view the items that are under History. From here, you can select the components you would like to delete. The top three are automatically selected, but you can select more, if you wish.

Tip #39: Do Not Track

Because every action you make online is being tracked by someone, it's always nice to be able to turn a feature like this off. Keep in mind that this feature will only request that the websites not track your activity, but it cannot enforce it. Most websites will respect your wishes, though. Ultimately, this is a great way to enhance your online privacy. To do this, open the Charms bar in Internet Explorer. Choose Settings and then Privacy, where you will see the Do Not Track option. Switch it to on if it is currently off. If you want to keep websites from tracking where you

live, turn the location tracking to off. Close IE
and re-launch it.

Chapter 6: Additional Valuable Tips

Last but not least, a chapter of a few more

helpful tips
that will make
your Windows
8 experience
much fuller.

Tip #40:
Keep App

Noise to a Minimum

Windows 8 applications will often alert you of
new e-mails, calendar events, messages, status
updates and more – very similar to that of your
smartphone. If you want to avoid these
notifications during certain times of the day, such
as overnight while you're asleep, you can create
special settings for Quiet Hours. In order to get
to where you can modify the settings, open up
the charms bar, select Settings, then Change PC
Settings and then Search and Apps. Here, you
will need to click on the Notifications subheading
on the left in order to open up the settings for
Quiet Hours.

Tip #41: Easily Share with the Share Charm

If you're browsing through your photos from this past weekend and find a photo that you must show off to all your friends on Facebook, pull up the Share Charm. You can then select the service (Facebook in this instance) and provide the name of a recipient(s), if you want, as well as a personal message. Then press Send and you've shared your photo with your friends! It saves a ton of time when compared to opening up the app or webpage itself, locating and uploading the photo and then sharing. Turn Quiet Hours on and select the desired time intervals. If desired, you can choose to only disable certain apps during this period and you can choose to receive or not to receive calls from your Skype app during this quiet period.

Tip #42: Live Tiles or Dead Tiles?

Live tiles provide real-time data on your Start Screen. There's no need to open the Weather app to find out the temperature outside and you don't have to open up the Mail app in order to see who your most recent e-mail is from, as it can all be seen from viewing the tile from your Start Screen. If you want to make a certain tile live, you can right click it and turn it on. The same is true for turning a Live tile off.

Tip #43: Turn Spell Check On or Off

 Windows 8 programs have an automatic spell-checking feature that works very similar to that of Microsoft Office. If a mistake is made in your typing, that annoying wavy red line will appear underneath. You can then right click or tap the word to see alternative suggestions. While most people find this helpful, some will obviously not. Therefore, if you would like to turn it off, simply pull up Settings from the Charms bar. Click on Change PC Settings and then PC and Devices. Select the subheading that says Typing. Make your modifications as you wish.

Tip #44: Where's the Volume?

Unless you're using the Desktop and not the Start Screen, you can't see the volume control down in the system tray, as neither is there. Instead you must open up the Charms bar, click on Settings and then click on Volume in order to adjust the volume. If you're on the Desktop version, then you shouldn't have a problem at all because the system tray is down in the bottom right corner just like it always has been in previous Windows versions.

Tip #45: Indispensable Gesture Commands

There are a number of new features with Windows 8, so don't feel bad if you have no idea what you're doing. While some may prefer to bring up the traditional desktop and do away with the new Windows 8 interface, if you can take the time and effort to learn these gesture commands, you will truly love the new interface – which honestly isn't as intimidating as you think it is.

Whether you want to use the mouse, keyboard or touch controls, here's a brief introduction into how to use some of these brand new features that Windows 8 has put at your disposal. (Keep in mind, this is sort of a refresher of some of the more popular and commonly used gestures that you'll use so that they are easily accessible within this eBook. These gestures have already been mentioned previously in the eBook and offered in much more detail than here.)

Opening the Charms Menu

Touch: Swipe from the right side edge of the screen for the Charms screen.

Mouse: Move your pointer to the corner of the screen (top or bottom will suffice) and wait a few seconds for the Charms menu to appear.

Keyboard: Press and hold down the Windows and C keys together for the Charms taskbar.

Switching Tasks

Touch: Swipe from the left side edge of the screen to show the very last app that was used. For all open apps, you'll want to swipe just a bit from the left and then back to the edge.

Mouse: Use the Windows and Tab keys with one another to quickly look through open apps.

Keyboard: Take your pointer to the middle of the left side screen. Click and drag the pointer for the next app to appear. For all open apps, go to the top or bottom screen corners and move to the center of the edge for the list of apps to show up.

Using Two Apps at the Same Time

Touch: Tap and drag the app to either side of the screen until you see a vertical bar.

Mouse: Point, click and drag the app to the left or right side of the screen. Alternatively, you can right click to open the context menu, where you can select "Snap Right" or "Snap Left".

Keyboard: For an app to be snapped to the right side of the screen, press the Windows and period key at the same time. For the left side, add in the Shift key so that you holding down the Windows, Period and Shift keys at the same time.

Closing Apps

Touch: Drag your finger from the top of the app screen down to the bottom of the screen until the app begins to disappear.

Mouse: Move your cursor to the top of the app screen until it turns into a distorted hand. Click and drag to the bottom until it begins to disappears

Keyboard: If you have an open app, you can still close it as you would on previous versions of Windows. Just use the ALT and F4 keys.

Open Options Menu

Touch: Simply swipe your finger up from the bottom of the screen.

Mouse: Right click on any empty space on the screen.

Keyboard: Press and hold the Windows and Z keys.

Chapter 7: Essential Hot Keys to Be

Familiar With

Hot keys are important to know, especially with Windows 8.

These hot keys will help you easily and quickly access several features of the new Windows 8 that you will use frequently.

Tip #46: Charm Bar Hot Keys

- Windows + C – Opens the Charms bar.
- Windows + I – Opens Settings.
- Windows + K – Opens Devices.
- Windows + H – Opens Share.
- Windows + Q – Opens Search.

Tip #47: Hot Keys to Get Around the Start Screen

- Left Arrow Key – Move to the left, one tile at a time.
- Right Arrow Key – Move to the right, one tile at a time.

- Up Arrow Key – Move up, one tile at a time.
- Down Arrow Key – Move down, one tile at a time.
- Home Key – Moves to the very first tile.
- End Key – Moves to the very last tile.
- Ctrl + Minus Sign (-) – Zooms out
- Ctrl + Equal Sign (=) – Zooms back in.

Tip #48: Hot Key Shortcuts for Apps

- Windows + Z – Displays the app bar in the current app or Start Screen.
- Windows + Tab – Opens a full list of the programs that are currently running.
- Windows + Period – Snaps your window to the left or right side and toggles when the period key is pressed.
- Windows + Shift + Period – Snaps active app to the left.
- Ctrl + Esc – Switches between the last app used and the Start Screen.
- Alt + Tab – In the centre window, cycles forward through the active apps.
- Alt + Shift + Tab – In the centre window, cycles backward through active apps.
- Alt + F4 – Closes the active app.

Tip #49: Hot Keys to Navigate the Desktop

- Windows + M – Minimizes all open apps and windows.
- Windows + Shift + M – Restores all previously minimized windows.
- Windows + T – Preview open apps and programs in the taskbar.
- Ctrl + N – In File Explorer, opens new window.
- Ctrl + W – In File Explorer, closes current window.
- Ctrl + Shift + N – in File Explorer, creates new folder.
- Alt + Esc – Toggle through open windows.
- Alt + F4 – Launches Shut Down menu.

Tip #50: Hot Keys to Access Helpful Features and Tools

- Ctrl + Shift + Esc – Opens up0020Task Manager for Windows.
- Windows + E – Opens up File Explorer.
- Windows + R – Opens up the Run command so that a command prompt can be used to launch apps and actions.
- Windows + U – Opens up the Ease of Access Centre.

- Windows + X – Opens up the Quick Access Menu/Power User Tasks Menu showing several system functions.

Tip #51: Additional Hot Keys You Need to Know

- Windows Key – Opens the Start screen with app tiles.
- Windows + Print Screen – Captures a shot of the screen and saves it in the corresponding folder.
- Windows + Down Volume – On a tablet, these keys will let you take a screenshot.
- Windows + Pause – Opens up the page of system properties showing your PC specs.
- Windows + Comma – All open windows will become transparent letting you see the desktop.
- Windows + D – From the Start screen, this takes you to the desktop.
- Windows + F – Opens up a folder and file search option.
- Windows + I – Opens up the settings menu allowing features such as Personalization and Control Panel to be easily accessed.
- Windows + L – Locks your computer so that it is secure when you walk away.
- Windows + O – Locks orientation computers and tablets that have an accelerometer.

- Windows + Q – Opens up a global search list of options.
- Windows + W – Opens up a search option for your system settings so that system properties can be easily located and changed.
- Windows + Plus Sign – Zoom in
- Windows + Minus Sign – Zoom out

Conclusion

As you have likely seen, Windows 8 is a bit of a complicated mess, especially if you aren't an internet wizard. However, the 50 tips outlined in this eBook will help you master Windows 8 and use it to your advantage. You should now be equipped with everything you need to know in order to truly get the hang of Windows 8 and take your user experience to the next level.